Maine

Scenes and Seasons

Maine

Scenes and Seasons

Photographs by Richard Procopio

Text by Mark Wanner

The New England Press
Shelburne, Vermont

Concept, text, and design © by The New England Press
Photographs © by Richard Procopio
All Rights Reserved
Designed by Andrea Gray
First Edition

ISBN 0-933050-95-X
Library of Congress Catalog Card Number: 92-81160

For additional copies or for a catalog
of our other titles, please write:
The New England Press
P.O. Box 575
Shelburne, Vermont 05482
Printed in Singapore
Through Four Colour Imports, Ltd,
Louisville, Kentucky.

Maine

by Mark Wanner

The State of Maine forms the northeast corner of the United States, and as a result, few people pass through it on their way to somewhere else. This makes Maine a destination unto itself, and it's the chosen destination of thousands of people each year. The many reasons are summed up on the residents' license plates—Maine is indeed Vacationland. It attracts presidents, movie directors, writers, and millionaires, as well as countless others who get less media attention. And Maine captures the imagination of just about everyone who visits it.

Perhaps the reason for Maine's appeal is that it's so full of contrasts. Some of the plushest resorts and restaurants in the East can be found along its coast, while the northern counties contain vast tracts of virtually untouched wilderness. Warm, sandy beaches are interspersed along its generally rugged, rocky coastline. The earliest sunrise in the country happens in Washington County, but it's countered by skies that darken well before 4:00 p.m. in the winter. And just about any outdoor recreation imaginable is available only a short trip away from an impressive array of shops and cultural attractions that can provide days of indoor exploration.

Many of the contrasts in Maine arise from its sheer size. People tend to forget just how big Maine is, especially those who stay near the southern coast. In fact, it covers 30,995 square miles—and one county alone, Aroostook ("The County," to the locals), is larger than Connecticut and Rhode Island combined. It's a long way from Kittery in the south to

Madawaska on the Canadian border in more ways than one—the climate, culture, and physical surroundings all change a lot along the way. And the side trips that beckon the traveler willing to leave the beaten path can take a lifetime to complete.

Even the coast, a modest 250-mile trip as the crow flies, becomes an odyssey of around three thousand miles if every inlet and peninsula is included. Small towns such as Harpswell, Boothbay Harbor, Stonington, and many others are situated at the end of long points of land and are surrounded on three sides by the Atlantic Ocean. The midcoast is particularly ragged—it looks like an unorganized jumble of land and water on the map. It's not too hard to figure out how to get around it, though, and journeys to the end of a spit of land are invariably rewarding.

Maine's coastline is its most recognized and most visited region, and its fame is well merited. At first glance, one might wonder why. After all, it's generally rugged and rocky, and the water never really warms up enough to allow for comfortable swimming (though there are always those hardy souls who refuse to be denied a bracing dip in the salt water). Any storm outside of deepest summer can make the whole shoreline quite inhospitable. Yet a visit to the Maine coast yields vistas of unexpected beauty, refreshingly cool breezes on hot days, and sandy beaches perfect for sunbathing. And after a day on the shore, there are ample opportunities to sample Maine's culinary specialty—a steaming, bright red, freshly caught lobster.

Summer is not the only time when people visit Maine. Wintertime Maine offers first-rate skiing, snowshoeing, and other winter activities, particularly in the western and northern counties. These areas are also renowned among outdoors enthusiasts for their excellent hiking, camping, hunting, and fishing. The farther north one heads, the wilder the countryside becomes. Large expanses of land remain untouched except by loggers and occasional hunting or fishing enthusiasts, particularly in Aroostook, Piscataquis, and Somerset counties. Most of the hardy inhabitants of Aroostook County live well north of Montreal, Canada. They take the harsh winters in stride, although the cold is truly punishing there at times—people who live farther south should check to see what temperature it is in Caribou, a favorite town of national weather forecasters, before they complain about the cold where they live!

History

EARLY HISTORY

Although Maine was admitted into the Union as the twenty-third state in 1820, European settlement of the area started some three hundred years earlier. John and Sebastian Cabot may have traveled far enough north to explore the Maine coast in 1498. Not surprisingly, they headed back south after taking a look at the chilly, rocky terrain. Subsequent explorers stayed to the south until 1603, when both the French and the English laid claim to the area. Still, claiming it for one's country was one thing—living there was another, as Sir John Popham found when he tried to establish a settlement at the mouth of the Kennebec River in 1607. He perished during the harsh winter, and the settlement was abandoned the next year. A permanent settlement was finally established in 1622, the year that the name Maine was originally used to distinguish between the mainland and the many nearby islands. During the 1620s and 1630s, several settlements were established along the southern coast, including one at what is now Portland. Although these settlements endured, Maine was unable to establish itself as an independent province, and it became part of Massachusetts in 1691. Despite problems brought about by its geographic isolation and severe attacks during the French and Indian and Revolutionary wars, Maine remained with Massachusetts for more than a hundred years, until discontent led to a separatist movement after the War of 1812. Residents voted for statehood in 1819 and gained it the next year.

MAINE AFTER STATEHOOD

After separating itself from Massachusetts, the new State of Maine faced a conflict with New Brunswick, the Canadian province that lies along the Aroostook River Valley on Maine's northern border. Although their common boundary had been disputed testily for several decades, the border situation came to a head in the late 1830s, when Canadians tried to claim territory in the area to control the potentially lucrative logging industry. Tempers reached the boiling point, and Maine residents joined forces to chase them out. The dispute is now called the Aroostook War but, thanks to the intervention of General Winfield Scott, no significant battles were fought. Maine and New Brunswick finally settled their dispute in 1842, resulting in the border that exists today.

Its status and shape established at last, Maine concentrated on building its economic strength. The timber industry, now freed from interference by New Brunswick lumberjacks, became a major economic force in the nineteenth century. Agriculture was also quite strong, which helped shape Maine's rural character. Today, although the techniques and products have changed and their relative importance has diminished, timber and agriculture are both still bedrocks of Maine's economy as suppliers to the state's major manufacturers. Fishing and shipping have always been less important to the overall economy, but they kept the coastal towns flourishing. The days of the sailing ships conjure up romantic images in most people's minds, and many people are drawn to the coast for a view of the fascinating remnants of Maine's maritime heyday.

Maine's population grew rapidly during the nineteenth century, but it slowed considerably in the twentieth, particularly in the cities. Right now, slightly more than a million people call Maine their home. Some of them still fish, pick blueberries, grow potatoes, and cut timber, but most hold down more typical modern-day jobs. A lot of residents work in Maine's tourism industry, the new economic force in the state, second only to manufacturing in overall income. Although their license plates say "Vacationland," Maine residents have to work hard to ensure that their state lives up to its billing.

Cultural Attractions

CITIES

If Maine cities were moved elsewhere in the United States, they'd probably be called towns. Yet as regional centers, they often have the facilities and atmosphere of cities much larger than they are. Portland, the largest, barely tops 60,000 people, although the figure approaches 200,000 if the surrounding communities are included. During the decade after Maine attained statehood, Portland was the state capital, and it has been a center of transportation, manufacturing, and fishing ever since. A piece of Portland's maritime history that can be seen today is the Old Port, an area near the waterfront that's currently popular for shopping and dining. Its narrow, cobbled streets are reminiscent of times past, but it's safe to say that the Old Port—once a notorious red-light district—is much nicer to visit today than it was then. Portland also boasts the Portland Museum of Art, which houses permanent collections of American and European art and exhibits special displays on a temporary basis. Other cultural highlights include the Wadsworth-Longfellow

House, the childhood home of poet Henry Wadsworth Longfellow; the Portland Observatory, a nineteenth-century signal tower; and the Tate House, a circa-1755 home with furnishings from that period. Physically active people enjoy jogging around Back Cove, a thirty-three-acre nature preserve located only minutes from the heart of downtown.

Maine's next largest cities are located in the interior of the state. Lewiston and Auburn lie opposite each other across the Androscoggin River, about thirty-five miles north of Portland. Although they are separate cities, they're closely linked in every way—when residents of Maine refer to "L.A.," they mean Lewiston-Auburn, and not any city in California. Together, they form a metropolitan area of nearly 75,000 residents. Lewiston and Auburn have been industrial centers since early in their history, and they remain so today. Lewiston is home to Bates College, a fine small liberal arts college founded in 1864.

Bangor, with more than 30,000 residents, lies along the Penobscot River, twenty-five miles from the coast. Although located in the southern half of the state, it's on the northern edge of the heavily populated area. Bangor was visited in 1604 by Samuel de Champlain, and it grew in the nineteenth century around shipping lumber and shipbuilding. Today, it's economy is based on manufacturing, and it also serves as a retail center for many residents of central Maine and the northeastern coast.

Augusta, astride the Kennebec River in the middle of southern Maine, is the state capital. It has served in that capacity since the end of Portland's brief tenure in the early nineteenth century. The striking Capitol is made of granite from nearby Hallowell. Those interested in an overview of Maine's history should visit Augusta's Maine State Museum, which houses displays and artifacts from years past. The original barracks of Fort Western, built in 1754 as protection against attacks by the French and Indians, is now a museum as well.

POINTS OF INTEREST

Most people who plan trips to Maine intend to leave the cities behind for at least a while and spend time outdoors in some way—on the coast, hiking, fishing, skiing, or whatever.

Unfortunately, the weather doesn't always cooperate with them, and there are many days when exploring a town or a museum is the perfect alternative to watching rain hit the windowpane or cars slowly turn into immobile ice blocks. Maine has many and diverse opportunities for indoor exploration outside its cities, and a comprehensive list of points of interest that merit at least a short visit would be far, far too long to include here. As a result, the following compilation merely touches upon a few of them around the state.

Along with Lewiston, Maine's primary college towns include Orono, Gorham, Waterville, and Brunswick. Orono, just north of Bangor, is home of the main campus of the University of Maine. Its satellite campuses are scattered throughout the state and provide high-quality education in towns such as Fort Kent and Machias. The twelve-thousand-student Orono campus offers strong programs in forestry, agriculture, and wildlife studies, in addition to traditional liberal arts subjects. The University of Southern Maine, the largest satellite campus, is in Gorham, just west of Portland.

Colby College, a small, selective liberal arts college, sits on a hilltop in Waterville, about halfway between Augusta and Bangor. Founded in 1813, Colby is the state's second oldest institution of higher learning. Bowdoin College, in Brunswick, is the oldest—it opened its doors to students in 1802. Bowdoin is also a highly regarded small liberal arts college, and Colby, Bates, and Bowdoin maintain fierce rivalries with one another in everything from football to blood-giving drives. Some competitions among them date back more than one hundred years. The Brunswick Naval Air Station, a large strategic naval base, is located just down the road from the college. Brunswick is also known for a variety of museums. Bowdoin has a well-regarded art museum as well as the Peary-MacMillan Arctic Museum. Admiral Peary, a Bowdoin alum, is thought to have been the first man to the reach the North Pole, though his claim is the subject of a lively debate. The Pejepscot Historical Society maintains two museums in town, including one in the home of Civil War hero Joshua Chamberlain. And Brunswick is where Harriet Beecher Stowe wrote *Uncle Tom's Cabin.*

Freeport, Brunswick's neighbor to the southwest, is a nationally known shopping mecca. L.L. Bean, the outdoor equipment and clothing outfitter whose catalogues are known far and wide, is the centerpiece of an impressive collection of outlet stores crammed into what is otherwise a small town. Freeport has only a small fraction of Maine's fine shops, however, so it's a good idea to keep a sharp eye out for unique merchandise anywhere in Maine. Inland from Freeport, the Shaker Museum in New Gloucester is a living museum in the oldest religious community in America. The Shakers are famous for their distinctive furniture and crafts, as well as the rather unusual rules of their faith.

Aroostook County is very wild, but even its northernmost edge provides an opportunity to view the area's past. The Acadian Village in Van Buren is just across the river from Canada and has sixteen reconstructed buildings that depict the life of early Acadian settlers. A little farther south, in Houlton, the Aroostook Historical and Art Museum displays early pioneer and Native American artifacts. This area is also known as one of the nation's leading potato producers. Idaho potatoes may be more prominently marketed, but nearly 10 percent of the nation's crop—three billion pounds or so—comes from Aroostook County. The schools still close each fall so that the students can help with the harvest. Fort Fairfield is the center of the potato industry and celebrates its boon with a Potato Blossom Festival in July. When the potato plants are in bloom, the green and white fields are indeed a sight to behold.

If all the history and economics lessons start to seem like work, not play, perhaps it's time to rub elbows—in spirit, at least—with some of Maine's celebrated present and former residents. The place to begin is, of course, Kennebunkport, the vacation home of George Bush. The media coverage of Kennebunkport has allowed more people than ever before to see the beauty of Maine and witness the excitement of fishing for bluefish. Before it became a presidential hideaway, Kennebunkport was best known for its beautiful rocky coast and stunning houses. Stephen King hails from Bangor—reading his books would make anyone think twice about heading up there, although most of the residents seem unperturbed. Campobello Island, off the easternmost tip of Maine, was the summer home of Franklin Delano Roosevelt. The Roosevelt Campobello International Park, jointly owned by the United States and Canada, contains the president's thirty-four-room "cottage," which is open to the public in the summer. The Carnegies, Rockefellers, and several other financially secure families used to maintain mansion-like summer homes in Bar Harbor during the first part of the century. In 1947 a devastating fire burned their summer homes and much of the rest of Bar Harbor to the ground.

The Coast

SUNBATHING AND BEACHCOMBING

Maine's coast is justly renowned for its rugged character. Nevertheless, it's dotted with excellent beaches, particularly along the southern coast. And although most of them are located relatively close to one another, there is a surprising variety of natural and man-made features among them. No matter which beach is chosen, however, it's a good idea to bring along some money—there's often a small fee for parking, even at seemingly remote areas. Bring some on-the-beach activities as well, as Maine's cold waters can swiftly discourage even the hardiest swimmers.

For those who enjoy a carnival atmosphere, Old Orchard Beach, located near Saco, is the biggest draw. Long a favorite with vacationers from Quebec (many signs near the beach are in French and English), Old Orchard Beach is one of the largest beaches on the entire Atlantic coast. All that space accommodates crowds of people who travel there during the summer. There are many shops and restaurants near the beach, as well as a small but well-equipped amusement park to entertain those who want to escape the sun and sand for a while. The beaches that dot the coast from York to Kennebunk are also quite popular. York, Ogunquit, Wells, and Kennebunk beaches are all near their respective towns' facilities, but even at the height of summer, they tend to have a quieter atmosphere than Old Orchard Beach.

Farther north the beaches get fewer and farther between, and it can take some driving to reach them. The midcoast has Popham Beach State Park and Reid State Park—both south of Bath—and Pemaquid Beach Park, south of Damariscotta. All three boast beautiful beaches that, while harder to reach than the southern beaches, offer more restful visits. All three are excellent beachcombing spots, too, because of the lack of nearby development. Although the far northern coast has little sand, it does have some popular pebble beaches. The one at Lamoine State Park lies just across Eastern Bay from Mount Desert Island and is an excellent place to see that island's mountains. Roque Bluffs State Park also contains a pebble beach, near the eastern edge of Washington County. Swimming here is sure to be quite a chilling experience any time of the year!

LIGHTHOUSES

Evoking the romance of the days when large ships sailed in and out of Maine's many harbors, lighthouses can be found all along the coast. During Maine's early days, ships often failed to safely navigate the many dangerous channels and rocks, but for the past two centuries the lighthouses have helped lessen the risk. A comprehensive tour of them would be exceedingly difficult. A number of them were built on islands—in fact, the Mount Desert Rock light, twenty-six miles off the coast, is the most isolated light in New England. But visiting a lighthouse that is accessible by car is a great way to spend an afternoon. Visitors are even permitted to climb the tower of some of them, and the views from the top are often spectacular.

Maine's first and perhaps its most famous lighthouse is the Portland Head Light, located near Cape Elizabeth. George Washington commissioned its construction, and it was completed in 1791. Pemaquid Point Light, in South Bristol, is also a popular destination. Overlooking a rather bleak and rocky section of the coast, the lighthouse itself is attractive and well-maintained. The former lighthouse keeper's house now contains the Fishermen's Museum, which displays tools used in the Maine fishing industry. The West Quoddy Head light, near Lubec, guards the easternmost point of the United States. Its unique red-and-white striped tower looks like a huge peppermint stick. Maine has many other lighthouses that can be reached quite easily, and all provide an excellent setting for photography, exploration, or simply quiet contemplation.

COASTAL TOWNS

Any town that lies on the coast has an obvious point of interest. To be sure, not all towns have beaches or lighthouses like the ones mentioned above, but many do have other attractions.

Bath, just east of Brunswick, is the home of the Bath Iron Works (BIW), a huge shipbuilding company that has constructed many important vessels for the United States Navy. From certain vantage points, BIW's impressive crane tower can be seen from miles away. Bath is also home to the Maine Maritime Museum, a large, multi-building museum that displays Maine's nautical heritage. Not only does it exhibit many artifacts from previous centuries, it shows the visitor boat-building in progress and provides boat rides on the Kennebec River, just upstream from where it empties into the Atlantic. Wiscasset, a few miles east, is worth a visit as well. It claims to be the prettiest village in Maine—a bold statement considering the stiff competition—and it is, indeed, very picturesque.

Camden nestles between the thirteen-hundred-foot Camden Hills and Penobscot Bay and, along with its southern neighbor Rockland, is a popular summer resort town. Camden is particularly famous for the large fleet of windjammers and schooners that sail in and out of its harbor. Some of these boats serve as northern cruise ships, providing a way to explore the coastline from the sea in splendor. A brisk hike to the top of Mount Battie offers a sweeping vista of Camden and Penobscot Bay from the other direction.

Boothbay Harbor, Stonington, and Belfast are also pretty harbor towns. Boothbay Harbor, on a spit of land south of Wiscasset, is a popular vacation area in the summer. It's right in the middle of the most intricate tangle of islands, coastal rivers, bays, and peninsulas along the coast, and the scenery is beautiful. Stonington is actually located on Deer Isle; getting there by car involves crossing a precarious-looking bridge. Those who don't like bridges are sure to hate this one! The town itself is small and much quieter than Boothbay Harbor, but it too is very scenic. Belfast looks out on Penobscot Bay from a relatively flat stretch of coast. The town straddles the Passagassawakeag River, the mouth of which serves as its harbor. Downtown Belfast is a nice spot for shopping, rest, and excellent views of northern Penobscot Bay.

Those with artistic tastes will enjoy Ogunquit, known for its theater, and Blue Hill, known for its pottery. York has an eighteenth-century jail and schoolhouse inland from its beach. In Wells, auto buffs will enjoy the Auto Museum, which houses a large collection of antique cars and other vehicles. Machias, on the northern coast, is the site of Burnham Tavern, the area's oldest building. It's furnished with Revolutionary War-era antiques and displays other artifacts from that time as well. Washington County's famous blueberry fields are nearby—they produce around nine out of every ten blueberries eaten in the United States. The bushes turn bright red in fall, giving entire fields a fiery appearance.

It's easy to fill a day's itinerary on any section of the Maine coast. In fact, some of the best days are spent with nothing more than a map, a car, and an open mind.

THE COAST OUTSIDE THE TOWNS

The many attractions on the coast of Maine draw thousands of people each summer. Bar Harbor, Portland Head Lighthouse, Boothbay Harbor, Old Orchard Beach, and Camden Hills, among others, deserve their popularity, and many visitors to Maine build their trips around one or more of them. But for those who want a quieter vacation or to escape traffic and crowds for a day or two, there are more than two thousand miles of coastline whose primary attraction is that there's nothing particularly noteworthy or famous in the vicinity.

In the midcoast, in particular, literally hundreds of side roads lead down to secluded coves and points of land. Exploring these points of land can take a surprisingly long time, so it's best not to set a strict itinerary. On a nice day, every other bend in the road seems to offer a picture-postcard scene. Even when the coast passes out of sight, the briny smell that pervades everything is a continual reminder that there's far more ocean than land nearby. Lobster boats crowd into harbors, and the stacks of lobster traps that line the shores aren't scheduled to be made into coffee tables quite yet. Water birds of all types fly or swim along the shore. Some of the best meals in Maine are prepared in small lobster "shacks" that seem to pop up in the middle of nowhere. They may be short on amenities, but the food they serve makes it easy to forget the spartan surroundings.

COASTAL PARKS

Unfortunately, it can be difficult to find a place to take a walk along the coast without crossing private property. Unguided walks along deserted bits of coastline aren't recommended unless there's some indication that visitors are welcome. A sure bet for a nice hiking trail and a seaside picnic is a state park. Parks with beaches or lighthouses—such as Two Lights State Park, Popham Beach State Park, and Reid State Park—tend to be busy during the summer. Parks that fit into a day designed to get away from the crowds can be found with a little effort, however. Moose Point State Park in Searsboro and Fort Point State Park in Stockton Springs are both small, pleasant, and relatively quiet. And for someone who really wants to leave the hustle and bustle behind, Warren Island State Park in Isleboro offers hiking, picnicking, and camping facilities about three miles east of Lincolnville. There's only one hitch—Warren Island can only be reached by boat.

The crown jewel of Maine's coastal parks is, of course, Acadia National Park. More people visit Acadia than any other national park except Yellowstone, and it's not at all difficult to understand why. There's yet another glorious view every few hundred feet, or so it seems, and a scenic combination of inland-like hills perched near spectacular coastline. Most of Acadia is located on Mount Desert Island, but it also encompasses a piece of the Schoodic Peninsula to the east and several nearby islands. Acadia offers excellent camping and other recreational facilities, but it's necessary to plan ahead. Information about how to plan a visit can be found in many guidebooks or by writing the Acadia National Park Superintendent.

Bar Harbor, the largest town on Mount Desert Island, is bordered on all sides by either Acadia or the ocean. It's popular in the summer, when whale watchers, travelers en route to Nova Scotia, visitors to Acadia, and other vacationers all converge on its shops and inns. Any Maine souvenir anyone could ever want can be bought along Main and Cottage streets, and there are plenty of places to kick back and enjoy an ice cream cone or soda. Summer fun is Bar Harbor's main attraction, but the town has a serious side too. It's the home of the College of the Atlantic, which, appropriately enough, specializes in marine studies. It's somewhat surprising to find in this holiday town Jackson Laboratory, a large scientific complex that is a world leader in mammalian genetics research. Jackson offers lectures and films about its work to the general public. Two other pretty towns, Northeast Harbor and Southwest Harbor, face each other across Somes Sound, on the southern edge of the Mount Desert Island. They're smaller and less hectic than Bar Harbor and retain more of an old-fashioned maritime atmosphere.

Inland Recreation

BAXTER STATE PARK

To anyone who enjoys outdoor activities, western and northern Maine is paradise on earth. Its colorful tapestry of mountains, lakes, rivers, and small towns beckons canoeists, hikers, fishermen, hunters, skiers, and other enthusiasts to leave their cares behind and enjoy some of the best spots in the East for their particular sport.

Any discussion of Maine's inland beauty must begin at Baxter State Park and its centerpiece, Mount Katahdin. Baxter covers two thousand acres of Piscataquis County and, in keeping with the wishes of former Maine governor Percival P. Baxter, has remained in pristine condition. Access by car is very limited, and other forms of transportation, such as canoes and hiking boots, are needed to explore the interior of the park. The nearby town of Millinocket is a popular staging area for hikers and campers preparing to leave modern comforts behind for a while. It's best to plan any trip to Baxter carefully. It's a wilderness area, so visitors must obtain and test their equipment and supplies ahead of time. Also, be sure to contact park officials well in advance of any planned trip.

Inside the park, networks of small ponds and streams cover the land to the north and southwest of the mountain. Beginning canoeists will find miles of excellent flatwater paddling on the small ponds, while experts can find navigable streams in favorable water conditions. The Nesowadnehunk Stream, on the western edge of the park, and the Wassataquoik Stream, in the east, are Baxter's major waterways, though the mighty West Branch of the Penobscot River just touches the southwest corner as it flows to the east. There are also dozens, perhaps hundreds of small mountain streams in the vicinity. Several campsites are located on the edges of ponds, including Daicey Pond in the south and Lower South Branch Pond in the north. The largest lake in Baxter is Grand Lake (Matagamon), on the northern edge, well away from Katahdin. Any pond is a good spot to look for moose, Baxter's most famous residents. These truly impressive animals often feed along the shore.

Hikers and other landlubbers can take advantage of a seventy-five-mile network of trails. Mount Katahdin is the hub of the network, but the trails take the hiker through all regions of the park. The most famous trail in Baxter, the Appalachian Trail, either begins or ends at Mount Katahdin, depending on one's point of view. The longest continuous hiking path in the world, it extends unbroken for more than two thousand miles to its other terminus in Georgia. By any trail, however, the climb to Katahdin's 5,267-foot summit (an even mile if the thirteen-foot tower on top is also included) is a challenging one. Near the top, the daring climber can hike along the Knife Edge, which looks like its name. The land falls away at perilously steep angles on either side of a ridge, whose width narrows to three or four feet in spots. Anyone who's the slightest bit scared of heights should think twice before taking this trail! Once at the top, the view is everything a tired hiker could hope for.

MOUNTAINS

Katahdin is Maine's highest and probably its best-known mountain, but there are many others that are worth climbing up or skiing down. The White Mountain National Forest extends from New Hampshire over Maine's western border, from Kezar Lake north to the Androscoggin River. Although the peaks in Maine's part of the forest aren't as high as those in New Hampshire's, several hiking trails in the park are perfect for day trips. North of the Androscoggin are Sunday River, a popular ski area, and Grafton Notch State Park, which has excellent hiking trails around 4,180-foot Old Speck Mountain. The Bear River, with its spectacular waterfalls and gorges, runs through the park. The town of Bethel, on the south bank of the Androscoggin, is the ideal spot to begin trips to all these areas.

Maine's largest ski area is Sugarloaf USA, way up in the northwestern corner of the state. Sugarloaf has all the amenities of a major winter resort on its 4,237-foot mountain, and nearby Kingfield is a typical ski town. Cross-country skiing enthusiasts gather at Carrabassett Valley, a large touring center down the road from the downhill skiing area.

Summer hikers will find trails on Sugarloaf Mountain itself and just to the north, in the Bigelow Mountain Preserve. Besides Sunday River and Sugarloaf, skiers can try Saddleback Mountain, near Rangeley, and Pleasant Mountain, between Bridgton and Fryeburg. For those who don't like venturing too far into the snowy countryside, Lost Valley, in Auburn, offers downhill skiing near Maine's second-largest metropolitan area.

These mountains are all relatively accessible, but there are also many mountain summits in places with names like T15 R9 and Twp 6. Any good hiking guide will describe the hikes in these areas, as well as any hazards or difficulties that might be encountered getting to and from them. For those who favor leisure and beauty over strenuous climbing, the autumn foliage is superb throughout Maine's mountainous areas. In countless places a short walk or drive will yield vistas with a dizzying variety of fall colors.

LAKES AND RIVERS

Maine has so many lakes and rivers that it's difficult to go far in any direction without running into one of them. And whether one is looking for a new whitewater kayaking challenge, a reliable fishing hole, or just a nice spot to dip a toe, it's easy to find the perfect place.

The Allagash River is heaven for experienced canoeists and campers. The center of the longest wilderness waterway in Maine, the Allagash branches off the St. John River near the U-shaped notch in northern Aroostook County and ends just west of Baxter State Park. In between, it meanders through an unspoiled series of lakes, rapids, and flatwater river stretches. Exploring the whole length of the Allagash and its side branches would take many trips, but there's no danger of tiring of the scenery in the area. Camping areas can be found along the shores over the entire route. A parallel trip can be taken on the St. John River to the west. It, too, winds through very remote country, but it's a straight-ahead whitewater river trip. It demands a great deal of paddling skill, and a guide is recommended.

Thrill seekers can find some of the country's finest whitewater rafting and kayaking along the Dead and Kennebec rivers and the West Branch of the Penobscot River. Several rafting companies lead daylong expeditions down the Kennebec and the Penobscot. The ride is wild at all times and is particularly hair-raising during the chilly spring runoff. The guides are all experts at guiding rafts safely down the river, however, so all the passengers have to do is grab a paddle, do what the guide says, and prepare for an exhilarating experience. Rafting schedules and other information are best obtained by contacting one of the rafting companies. The heaviest sections of whitewater are best left to experienced rafters, but kayakers and whitewater canoeists can find runnable stretches elsewhere on both rivers. The Dead River north of Rangeley is another favorite spot for experienced whitewater enthusiasts.

More placid boating experiences can be had on Maine's many lakes. Some of the best fishing in the East is found in these lakes as well—any good fishing guide will describe where to go to catch different kinds of game fish. Many of the northern lakes are still completely undeveloped and inaccessible except by boat or plane. Farther south, lakeside development tends to be very restrained and unobtrusive. Nonetheless, visitors will find some amenities, like solid roofs, that can be very nice to have—especially considering Maine's fickle weather!

Huge Moosehead Lake, west of Baxter State Park, offers visitors a little bit of comfort and a lot of wilderness. Greenville, right on the lake's southern tip, has long been a popular base of operations for those exploring the Moosehead area and is easily accessible by car. Many guides are based in Greenville and nearby Rockwood, and one should be contacted before attempting any serious exploration of the area. Flight services can be found in Greenville—away from town, almost every other part of the lake's ragged shoreline can be reached only by boat or plane. Aside from numerous small campsites, the shoreline and surrounding areas are very wild. A favorite stop on the way to the northern part of Moosehead is Mount Kineo, which rises steeply to a summit 1,789 feet above the lake. Other wild yet accessible spots are Rangeley Lake and nearby Cupsuptic and Mooselookmeguntic lakes, which lie just east of the northern tip of New Hampshire. Nearby Saddleback Ski Area makes this a true four-season recreation area.

The southern interior is dominated by Sebago Lake, halfway between New Hampshire and the coast at Freeport. Sebago is twelve miles long, up to eight miles wide, and reaches depths of four hundred feet. It's very popular with fishermen—especially those in pursuit of landlocked salmon—and summer vacationers. It's connected to the north with Long Lake, via the Songo Lock. The pretty town of Naples sits on the southern end of Long Lake. The Belgrade Lakes, a collection of smaller lakes north of Augusta and west of Waterville, are known for their bass fishing and are quite easily reached for a relaxing afternoon in a canoe.

Conclusion

It would take hundreds of pages to describe all the places in Maine that are worth visiting. The short descriptions given here and the beautiful photographs that follow merely provide a glimpse of the beauty and history within Maine's borders. Even though there's too much to see and do in any one visit, there's always an excuse to come back to explore Maine a little more.

Wells Beach *(opposite)*

Harvest Time

Kennebunkport

Pemaquid Point Light

West Branch of the Penobscot River

Portland Skyline (*overleaf*)

Mackerel Cove

Megunticook Lake *(opposite)*

Lobster Crates

The Capitol, Augusta

Cape Porpoise

Union Fair

Sailing near Port Clyde

Screw Auger Falls *(opposite)*
Mount Katahdin from Sandy Stream Pond (*overleaf*)

Monhegan Island Volunteer Fire Department

Portland Head Light

Washington County Blueberries

Otter Cliff, Acadia National Park

Potato Harvest in Aroostook County

Vinalhaven

Cemetery Flowers

Fog on the Coast *(opposite)*
Bar Harbor and the Porcupine Islands from Cadillac Mountain *(overleaf)*

Sunrise at Daicey Pond

Winter Lobstering

Schooner Festival in Boothbay Harbor

Cross-Country Skiing *(opposite)*

Coastal Scene, York

Bull Moose

Schoodic Point

Lovejoy Covered Bridge, Andover *(opposite)*
Fall Foliage in Rangeley *(overleaf)*

Cape Neddick Light

Fisherman on Mousam River *(opposite)*

Swift River, Roxbury

Ash Point

Wave Watching

Winter on the Farm

Rafting on the Kennebec River

Marshall Point Light

Canoes on South Branch Pond, Baxter State Park (*overleaf*)

Christmas at Tenants Harbor

The Pier at Old Orchard Beach

Inland Waters, Acadia National Park

Fly Fishing on the Kennebec River

Massachusetts Hall, Bowdoin College

Spruce Woods

Fishing Shanty on Moosehead Lake

Portland

Foliage near Kingfield

The Beehive, Acadia National Park *(opposite)*
Chasing Rainbows *(overleaf)*